Worm Farming Made Simple

THE DEFINITIVE GUIDE TO WORM FARMING

PYLAN DESKINS

Table of Contents

CHAPTER 1

Worm Farming Made Simple:

The Definitive Guide to Vermicomposting

A great way to recycle kitchen waste and food scraps into one of the best garden fertilizers is by using worm farms!

A worm farm can be set up in the tiniest of spaces, such as balconies and courtyards, and it requires very little time and effort to maintain.

The term "worm farm" refers to a vermicomposting system, and earthworms are among the most efficient composters on the planet.

We'll go over how worm farms work, how to set one up, and how to maintain it in this article.

How to Select a Worm Farming Company

When it comes to purchasing or building your own worm farm, there are many options to choose from.

Stacks of trays with legs are the most common form of worm farms, and they don't take up a lot of space. Size-wise, they are ideal for a small home.

If you're looking for a larger worm farming system, such as a wheelie bin worm farm, that can process large amounts of food waste, you can build one out of an old bathtub. Large families, schools, cafes, restaurants, and workplaces in general can benefit from these larger worm farms.

Choosing a worm farm that will fit in your available space and can handle the volume of food waste you generate is critical.

.

The 'footprint,' or the amount of ground the worm farm consumes, should be taken into account. Three worm farms take up a fair amount of space in my backyard, which is fortunate because it's in an otherwise unused area. As time went on, I started with one worm farm, then two, and then three – it wasn't planned to run three of them side-by-side!

The capacity of a bathtub worm farm is about 200 liters, and it takes up about the same amount of space as a bathtub.

Wheelie-bin worm farms can hold 140 liters, 240 liters, or 360 liters of worms and take up very little ground space. Due to its wheeled design, it can be easily moved around. Worm farms last a long time and are a great investment for organic gardeners, so think about what you need before you buy.

Where Do the Worms Come From in a Worm Farm?

When food scraps are broken down by earthworms, they produce worm casting and worm casting leachate, which is better known as 'worm wee.'

An early photo of the worm farm 'before' shows a mix of fresh scraps and those in various stages of decomposition.

Since converting organic matter into usable worm castings is a task that can be accomplished by any type of earthworm, we naturally opt for the best-performing worms for the job.

Compost worms, as opposed to the common earthworms found in garden soil, are the type of earthworms commonly used in worm farms. In contrast to garden earthworms, compost worms are surface feeders and do not penetrate the soil as far as garden earthworms. It's not uncommon for different compost worm species to consume their own body weight in food each day. That means that one pound of worms will eat that much food every day! It takes garden earthworms longer to break down large amounts of material because they only eat half of their body weight each day.

Remember that compost worms will not survive in the soil of your garden. In the heat of summer, they can't go deep into the ground like regular earthworms because they're surface feeders, so they die quickly. Composting organic material on top of the soil is also necessary for them to feed, so if you don't have any organic matter decomposing on top of your soil, they won't have any food.

They are all decomposers, which means they eat rotting organic matter and excrete it in the form of worm castings. They must wait for their food to break down before they can eat it because earthworms lack teeth. The worms can eat their food more quickly if it is chopped or broken into smaller pieces.

CHAPTER 2

Having covered the basics of earthworm theory, we can now move on to discussing worm farm layouts in more detail.

Two stacked trays are commonly used to construct a worm farm:

Worms and food scraps are kept in the upper tray.

Air holes in the lid keep pests at bay while allowing worms to breathe.

Any liquid can be drained away through the holes in the bottom.

• The liquid that drips from the top tray is collected in the bottom tray.

A tap or outlet on one side allows the liquid to be drained from the device. •

The bottom tray's liner prevents the worms from falling into the liquid below through the drain holes and drowning. As a liner, a piece of cardboard or newspaper works well in commercial worm farms. Use a piece of shade-cloth or window screening first in homemade worm farms, where the drain holes are larger, before laying down a layer of cardboard or newspaper on top.

The worms' home is a damp layer of coconut coir, but other materials, such as damp shredded newspaper or well-aged compost or manure, can be used as worm bedding as well.

We'll go into more detail about what you can and can't feed your worms later on in this article about what food scraps you can feed your worms.

Worm blankets can be made from an old hessian sack or even a whole newspaper, and they help create a dark, comfortable climate by keeping their bedding and food moist and cool. This makes it easier for them to eat their food. Because it is biodegradable, the cover will disintegrate in a few weeks' time.

There are a few variations on this basic worm farm design. When the top tray of your worm farm fills up with worm castings, you can simply add another tray on top of it and start adding kitchen scraps, and the worms will move up to the food. This is the general idea behind most worm farms that you can buy. While the worms are eating in the new tray, the lower tray of finished castings can be removed and used in the garden.

A different worm farm design will be examined to see if it also works.

How to Make a Worm Farm in a Bathtub

When it comes to large-scale worm farms made from recycled bath tubs, there are only one or two levels.

Traditionally, a bathtub is elevated off the ground using bricks or a wooden stand or frame, and water is collected in a bucket below the drain hole. To ensure that only liquid escapes, a mesh or screen covers the drain hole.

Using coarse gravel for drainage, the bottom of the bathtub is lined with shade cloth, and then bedding material is added to the bath. The rest of the worm farm is a typical structure with the same basic layers.

In order to keep the worms from overheating, a timber sheet or wooden cover is used.

Design for an in-bath worm farm

A worm farm built out of a recycled bathtub and a steel frame from a recycled dog bed!

Choosing the right location for a worm farm can make all the difference. In order to keep your worms happy, you should place the worm farm in the shade, away from direct sunlight, so that it does not overheat.

As long as it doesn't get too hot inside, you can put the worm farm in a shed or garage, as long as it's shady and doesn't get too hot in there during the summer. You can also use a well-protected area of a balcony.

If you want to keep your worm farm close to your kitchen, which will be the source of the food scraps you feed it, make sure you place the worm farm close by. You're less likely to use your worm farm if it's difficult to get to.

In the kitchen, you can keep a small bucket or container with a lid to dispose of your food scraps. When you're done, empty it into the worm farm. To keep the container clean, line it with a piece of newspaper. The newspaper will decompose in the worm farm along with the food scraps.

In order to start a worm farm, here are the seven steps:

Assemble a purchased worm farm or build a worm farm from scratch. 1. (see instructions for building a worm farm here).

Make sure the top tray is lined with about 0.5cm (1/4") thick newspaper or a sheet of cardboard.

You can use a moistened container of compost or aged manure instead of buying bedding material, which you can then place on top of the liner in the tray at the top.

To keep worms out of the bedding, use a damp newspaper or a hessian sack as a cover.

CHAPTER 3

A good starting point is 500-1,000 worms, but you can increase the number of worms if you prefer.

During this time, the worms will be adjusting to their new surroundings.

Feed the worms sparingly after a few days.

Choosing a Worm Food

First and foremost, pay attention to what you feed your worms. Worms won't eat certain things, and it's unhygienic to put them in a worm farm in the first place.

If you're not familiar with the vermicomposting process, keep in mind that worm farms are designed to break down food scraps quickly. The slow decomposition of woody garden trimmings and green waste necessitates the use of a regular compost bin.

What can and cannot be included in your worm farm?

The things you can add to your worm farm

• Vegetable and fruit scraps

• Cheese and bread

There will be no meat-based sauces in this section of the menu. • Cooked vegetables, grains, pasta, and rice.

If the teabags are made of paper and not plastic mesh, coffee grounds and teabags are acceptable.

A good source of calcium, which worms need to stay healthy, is found in eggshells.

There are no glossy printed pages on the newspaper and unprinted cardboard (soaked).

Things You Can Put In Your Worm Farm (With Caution!)

• Vacuum cleaner dust – only if your carpets are natural fibre, not synthetic carpets!

• Only use a small amount of citrus and onions, or none at all!

- Pet waste – only in a dedicated worm farm for pet waste only

Worm Farm Contaminants You Shouldn't Include

Fish and meat should be composted in a Bokashi bin to keep rats and other vermin away.

Instead of putting garden waste in a worm farm, put it in a compost bin.

Paper that is shiny and bleached is toxic, and you don't want it near your garden.

There are many vermicides in fresh manure, so compost them before using them in your garden. — worms

Feeding Your Worms the Right Way

Second, the method by which you feed your worms is extremely significant as well.

If you need to fold a damp hessian sack or an entire

newspaper to fit the bedding, you can do so by placing the food on the bedding beneath the 'worm blanket'.

You should start with a small amount of food in your worm farm and increase the amount as the worms begin to feed after a few days. Inadequate feeding of your worms leads to food going uneaten and eventually rotting, making your worms' environment unhealthy.

Put food on one side only, and try to cover at least half of that side at the most when feeding the worms in a worm farm. To be safe, you can always move the worms to the other side of the worm farm where there isn't any food. They'll have nowhere else to go if they don't like your latest food offering if you completely cover it up. After they've eaten the food on one side, switch to the other side and repeat the process until there is always a food-free side available.

The worm farm's worm population will increase as the

worms breed. Food consumption will increase as they grow, allowing you to keep adding more. When the number of worms in the worm farm and the food available has self-regulated to match, you'll know exactly how much food they can handle.

Worm Farm Leachate: How to Collect and Use It

Wee, the byproduct of worm casting, is like liquid gold for your garden.

The liquid that seeps out of a worm farm is commonly referred to as "worm wee" or "worm pee," but it is actually known as worm casting leachate.

To collect the leachate, follow these steps:

Alternatively, you can fill a bucket with the liquid from your worm farm's tap by placing a bucket under the tap and turning it on. Close the tap once you've collected all of the water.

CHAPTER 4

There should be an outlet (a pipe) in the bottom of the worm farm for the liquid, so place a small bucket there to collect the liquid as it comes out.

Flooding can be avoided by simply leaving your worm farm's tap open and placing a bucket underneath it. This is how I prefer to do it, and you can see the bucket filling up after a light rain in the picture above.

To use the leachate on your garden, first dilute it with water. Otherwise, it may be too strong.

In other words, use one part of the leachate for every ten parts of water when diluting this solution. It will take on the color of weak tea when it is diluted.

To avoid confusion, it's important to remember that the leachate isn't a fertilizer in the traditional sense, but rather a nutrient-rich soil conditioner that improves the health of the soil. Consider it more of a food for the soil and plants than a dietary supplement. You should always dilute it with rainwater because tap water is chlorinated and will kill all the beneficial microorganisms in it!

Worm Castings: How to Collect and Use

A worm castings pile is ready for collection when the bedding material and food scraps have decomposed to a dark, rich, fine, moist substance that can no longer be distinguished from the rest of the pile.

The best time to collect the castings is in the spring and fall, when fertilizing your garden is most effective.

The most difficult part of collecting worm castings is to separate the worms from the castings!! Keeping your worms in the worm farm is what you want to do. We'll go over a few methods for harvesting worm castings and separating the worms in more depth later on.

Worms from Castings: A Step-by-Step Guide

The 'Rainy Day' Method

If you have a stacked tray worm farm, you can wait for a day when it looks like it's going to rain before you start your worm farming operation. For this reason, worms rise to the surface when there is rain in an effort to avoid drowning when it rains heavily. When the rain floods their burrows and tunnels in the ground, this is a natural survival instinct.

Upon reaching the top, all of the worms in the lower tray will disperse and congregate in the top tray or the lid's inner cavity. You can quickly remove the lower tray and store it for later use once they've all risen. The bacteria in the soil will be washed away if you leave it out in the rain. Instead, keep it dry and use it in the garden right away after the rain has passed.

Don't leave the castings in a bucket for an extended period of time because there is no drainage and any moisture at the bottom may become stagnant water in worm farms with a bottom door to harvest castings.

The "Pyramid" Method

So, what do you do if you need castings but it isn't going to rain any time soon? We can also take advantage of worms' dislike of light, so avoid placing them in direct sunlight when caring for them. Worms burn easily in direct sunlight.

Wear rubber gloves and put on a low flat container or board and shape it into an inverted pyramid to separate worms from the castings you've collected. Use a well-ventilated area outside for this.

To avoid the light, the worms will burrow downwards rather than remain in the narrow pointed tip. When you're done with that, put the rest in an empty bucket. Afterwards, create a new pyramid out of the pile and collect the worm-free castings once more. In time, the pyramid will shrink, and the worms will continue to move toward the bottom. Put the worms back in the worm farm when you have a small, flat pile of worms.

CHAPTER 5

Involving Worms in Decision-Making

It's possible to use yet another of the worm's natural instincts in order to expedite the harvesting of castings. They'll be forced to live in their own waste if their bedding turns to castings, and that's not how they want to live. They prefer to sleep on clean sheets and have access to food.

You can make a fresh bedding area in your worm farm by pushing the castings to one side of the worm farm, putting fresh bedding in that space, and only laying food on that fresh bedding side. The worms will then move over to the fresh bedding area. This is when you can go ahead and collect all of the castings because they will have finished eating all of the food in the nicer side. In worm farms that are long and wide, such as bathtub worm farms, this method works well.

You may come across earthworm eggs or cocoons while collecting worm castings. Lemon-shaped amber or yellow eggs about 3mm (1/8") in diameter can be identified easily because they look like beads, but if you look closely enough, the shape of the lemons can be seen in the closer inspection. Recycle these worms as soon as possible if you find them.

To get the most out of your castings, use them as soon as possible after collecting them. Don't let them sit around for too long or let them dry out.

There are a plethora of applications for your castings now that you've gathered them.

Using Worm Castings: A Quick Guide

Dig into the soil or put it under mulch in the garden.

Make sure your seed-raising medium contains up to 25% worm castings before sowing your seeds.

add to potting soil during the growing season for houseplants

Worm castings are an excellent compost activator because they introduce beneficial bacteria that will help your compost get off to a faster start.

It can be sprayed on leaves or watered into the soil like compost tea. Worm casting tea is rich in nutrients and soil-beneficial microorganisms.

Worm castings can be used in the same way as any other slow-release organic fertilizer.

This article does not include instructions on how to make worm casting tea (or compost tea), which is a process that would take an entire article to describe.

Worm Farm Problems Solved

There are a few things to keep in mind when it comes to caring for your worm farm that will make it much easier. Listed here are a few of the most common issues you may encounter, as well as some simple solutions.

How to Keep Rain Out of Worm Farms

If your worm farm isn't covered, it will get rained on, and depending on the design, some rainwater will make its way in. You can use the leachate from the worm castings (worm wee) in your garden as it flushes out the castings and makes a good supply of the material.

It is possible that your worm farm will be flooded if it has a tap but it is closed.

The simplest solution is to place a small bucket under the tap and leave it open all the time, as shown in the illustration below. This prevents the tap from becoming clogged as well.

Prevent flooding by leaving the tap open and placing a bucket underneath!

If you must leave the tap closed, provide worms with a 'island' they can climb on if they fall into the liquid at the bottom. Place a terracotta pot upside-down in the worm farm's liquid collection area. In order to keep the worms from escaping the terracotta pot's sloped sides, the pot is heavy enough and the surface isn't as slippery as plastic, as shown below.

Use a terracotta pot 'island' inverted to keep your worms from drowning.

Make sure to open the tap and take out the liquid once a week from your worm farm, as well as immediately after a rainstorm if your farm is exposed.

Keeping Worm Farms Cool in Extreme Heat

Accidentally allowing worms to overheat in hot weather is the quickest way to kill off an entire worm farm's population.

The location of the worm farm has already been discussed in this article, and it should be in a shaded, protected area away from direct sunlight. Due to direct sunlight or hot west afternoon sun coming from sideways, even the shadiest spots can be exposed to direct sunlight in summer.

When it is hot outside, the worm farm can overheat because it is enclosed in a container, which traps the heat from the outside. Allow the worm farm lid to be slightly propped open to allow for better air circulation and the release of any hot air that may be accumulating underneath. Put a stick across the worm farm's top and cover it with the lid, leaving a gap between the worm farm's top edge and the lid.

You may need to use a watering can and rainwater to cool down the worm farm on extremely hot days. It's important to keep the worms' environment dark and moist by covering the bedding and food with a "worm blanket," such as newspaper.

To avoid flooding, open the faucet and place a bucket under it to catch the water. If you use a watering can, make sure to wet the entire surface evenly. Tap water contains chlorine, which can kill many of the beneficial bacteria in your worm farm, so avoid it if you can! Wetting the bedding and cover material with water creates a slow evaporation process that cools down the worms.

CHAPTER 6

A screen of some kind that is light-colored and will reflect the sun is the best way to shield worm farms from direct heat; make sure that the screen has enough space underneath it to prevent hot air from being trapped over the worm farms and leading to overheating. During the cooler months, simply remove the screen and replace it with a new one.

There is no better way to ventilate the worm farms than by using cheap reflective plastic sheeting that is suspended high above the worm farms. In order to keep the tarp in place, you can secure its bottom to a brick or other heavy object.

My worm farms (and compost bin on the far left) are shown here, safely enclosed by a fence.

Without a shelter, worm farms in the colder months

With lids slightly open and a reflective plastic tarp sheet covering, worm farms stay cool during the hot seasons.

Managing Worm Farm Insects

Having a few other insects in your worm farm is perfectly normal, but some of them are not welcome.

Worm farms aren't good places for ants, and this may be because ants prefer dry environments, which your worm farm lacks.

A watering can full of rainwater can be used to dampen down the worm farm and create an ant moat by placing the legs of your worm farm (if it has legs) in a tray of water.

The legs of the worm farm sit in plastic pot trays filled with water, forming a moat to keep ants out!

On hot days, remember to keep your water supply topped off. The idea of using oil-filled containers that don't evaporate has been floated, but I believe that will result in a disgusting muck as dirt is blown in on the breeze. My opinion is that water is a better solution!

Another option is to apply Vaseline to the legs of a worm farm, but this will likely melt in warm climates.

In general, ants aren't an issue unless you overfeed your worm farm with sugary food, which can attract ants if the food has been there long enough to attract them. To speed up digestion, chop the food into smaller pieces!

When you lift the lid of a compost bin or worm farm, vinegar flies will fly up into your face. You can prevent them from breeding by covering the food scraps with a damp newspaper (remember that all-important 'worm blanket' cover over your bedding) and preventing the food from rotting.

Insects such as millipedes, which feed on decaying organic matter, aren't a problem because they decompose and return the nutrients to the soil. Other names for slaters include "butcher boys" and "pillbugs."

Slaters are land-based crustaceans that aid in the decomposition process. Despite their unsettling appearance, soldier fly larvae, which resemble enormous silver-grey maggots, are an important part of the ecosystem. As well as being easily identifiable as the hopping insects that appear on top of a container when the lid is lifted, springtails play an important role in Earth's recycling ecosystems as members of the decomposer community.

If you see tiny white worms in your worm farm, they aren't baby earthworms; instead, they are entrachyadids, which aren't harmful but do indicate that your worm farm's pH has risen a tad above normal. Alkalize your worm farm by adding a small amount of garden lime, dolomite, or wood ash on a regular basis.

Worm Farm Odors and How to Get Rid of Smelly Worms

A worm farm that is in good health will have a pleasant earthy smell, similar to that of healthy soil or a forest floor, but it will not be overpowering. You can correct the problem by adding crushed eggshells, garden lime, dolomite, or wood ash to the mix.

If it has a strong odor, your body's oxygen supply has been compromised due to an abundance of undigested food. Stop adding food to the compost pile, add some garden lime, dolomite, or wood ash, and lightly stir the existing food scraps on a regular basis to aerate them. The worms can be fed again as soon as the smell subsides.

Conclusion

As you can see, running a worm farm is simple and doesn't require a lot of time or effort.

What your plants will appreciate most is the free supply of valuable castings and leachate you'll get from the worm farm.

To begin worm farming, it's time!

THE END